PICTURE HISTORY

FARMING
in History

PICTURE HISTORY

CLOTHES
EXPLORATION
FARMING
FOOD
HOMES
LANDSCAPE
MACHINERY
RECREATION
RELIGION
SCHOOLS
SHOPS
TRANSPORT
WARFARE

PICTURE HISTORY
FARMING
IN HISTORY

Ralph Whitlock

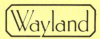

First published in 1983 by
Wayland Publishers Limited
49 Lansdowne Place, Hove
East Sussex BN3 1HF, England

© Copyright 1983 Wayland Publishers Ltd

ISBN 0 85078 357 7

Series Design by Behram Kapadia

Phototypeset by Kalligraphics Ltd, Redhill, Surrey
Printed in Italy by G. Canale & C.S.p.A., Turin
Bound in the U.K. by The Pitman Press, Bath

Contents

Introduction	9
The Farming Year	10/11
A Medieval Manor Farm	12/13
A Poor Man's Farm	14/15
Shearing the Flock	16/17
Monasteries	18/19
Serving his Lordship	20/21
Harvesting Fruit	22/23
Bringing Corn to the Mill	24/25
A Busy Farmyard	26/27
A Swarm of Bees in May	28/29
Jethro Tull	30/31
The First Agricultural Show	32/33
The Beginning of Automation	34/35
McCormick's Reaper	36/37
A Farmhouse Dairy	38/39
The Autumn Round-up	40/41
Cotton Plantations	42/43
The Agricultural Union	44/45
London's Meat Market	46/47
Beer – the Poor Man's Drink	48/49
Haymaking in Summer	50/51
Holidays in the Hop-fields	52/53
Farewell to the Horse	54/55
Farming Becomes Mechanized	56/57
Acknowledgements and Sources of Pictures	58
Sources of Further Information	60
Glossary	61
Index	62

Introduction

Have you ever lived on a farm? Your great-great-great-grandfather almost certainly did. He had to. Until only a few hundred years ago nearly everybody lived on farms.

This book describes what they grew, what animals they kept, how they set about doing their work and how they lived their lives.

In northern countries summer is short. Crops must be encouraged to grow as quickly as possible. Around the time of the spring equinox, which is March 21st when the day and night are of equal length, everyone got busy sowing seed.

In spring, too, grass began to grow. All through the spring and summer there was plenty of food for animals which eat grass. These are cows, sheep, horses and geese. Pigs need grain, meal and roots; and poultry need grain.

In summer farmers would think about how they were going to feed their animals during the coming winter. So they cut long grass and stored it as hay.

In August and September the grain crops ripened, and they had to be cut, too. Then they were threshed to extract the grain, which was taken to the miller for grinding.

In autumn the farmer counted his farm animals, took stock of his stores of food and decided how many he could keep during the winter. The surplus animals were either sold or killed. Those which were killed were salted down, so that the meat would keep through the winter.

Throughout the year sheep as well as cows were milked. Some of the milk was drunk but much more was made into cheese or butter.

So, when the summers were good and the crops prospered, our ancestors lived quite well. They had bread, cheese, butter, milk, eggs, oatmeal for porridge, meat, vegetables and fruit. Often the local water supply (from wells or ponds) was polluted, so everyone, even children, drank ale, made from barley.

One thing they lacked was sugar. Instead, they had honey. Bees were much more commonly kept in those days. Almost every farm had its hives of bees, and a special beekeeper to look after them.

This book describes how people set about producing their food, and their clothes and other necessities as well, in the centuries before they could go to a shop and buy them. It tells how, from the simplest tools and methods to start with, men developed improved tools, learned how to grow better crops and kept better animals. The improvements are still going on. but our food still comes from farms, though much of it goes through factory processes before it arrives, neatly packed, in our homes.

The Farming Year

These pictures show farmers at work in the eleventh century, about the time when William the Conqueror invaded England. In those days nearly everybody lived in villages and worked on farms. They had to, because there were almost no shops. If they did not grow their own food they starved.

In autumn and winter they had to plough the soil in readiness for sowing.

The ploughman is using a heavy wooden plough, drawn by four oxen. The ground is very rough, and the oxen have to pull hard to keep the plough moving. The man on the left is prodding them with a sharp-pointed stick, called a goad. He is probably a slave because, unlike the ploughman, he is not wearing shoes. The man on the right is sprinkling something on the soil. It is probably pigeon-dung or poultry-dung. Even in those days farmers knew that this was valuable fertilizer.

Sowing the Seed

March is the month for sowing. When the winter frosts were over and March winds were drying the soil, the people set about levelling the fields, to make them fine and smooth for sowing the seed. The man on the left is wielding a mattock, for breaking up clods. The next man is busy with a spade. At the right of the picture a man is sowing seed, probably barley. His neighbour is raking the seed into the ground, so as to bury it before birds can eat it.

All through the summer the crops growing in the fields have to be kept free from weeds and protected against birds and animals. At last in August the corn ripens and is ready for harvest.

Reaping the Harvest

So many people worked in the harvest fields that they needed a supervisor to organize them. He is the man on the left, blowing his horn as a signal to the harvesters to start work. The reapers are cutting the standing corn with sickles, or reap-hooks. Only one reaper is shown here but there would have been ten or twenty, working side by side.

When each has cut a handful he hands it to another man, who collects the stalks into bundles or sheaves. He uses twisted straw to tie them. Other men are carrying the sheaves to a cart, where a man with a prong is loading them. The cart has wooden wheels and sides of wickerwork or hurdles. When it is full, oxen or perhaps men, will pull it to the rickyard.

Later, when harvest is over, the sheaves will be threshed by men with flails. The grain will be taken to the mill, for the miller to grind into flour. Then women will make the flour into loaves and bake them.

A Medieval Manor Farm

This is a farmyard scene from the Middle Ages, perhaps three hundred years later than the previous one. It shows a manor farm, belonging to a wealthy man.

The Year in a Picture

The artist has been so eager to fit in everything that he has forgotten what season it is! As there are no leaves on the trees, it should be winter, but the sower would be at work only in autumn or spring. Those curious creatures like spiders, scrambling over the roofs in the background, are supposed to be bees, and they are swarming, which happens only in summer.

Let us look at the details. In the foreground the plough appears to be similar to the one of the eleventh century, but it is being pulled by horses instead of by oxen. Behind them is another horse, drawing a harrow. The harrow is a triangular timber frame studded with iron spikes. It does the work that in the first picture was being done by the men with mattock, spade and rake. On the other side of the fence, which is made of hurdles, are more horses. These are much better and bigger animals than the ones harnessed to the plough and the harrow. They are riding horses, bred to carry a knight dressed in armour.

Next to the riding horses are the cows. They look rather lean but that is partly because they are old. Cows were kept for doing farm work. They gave very little milk, and when they were too old for work they were killed for meat.

The sheep, which come next, are, of course, not drawn in proper proportion. They are not really as big as the cows. They are kept for wool and meat but also for milk.

Artificial Thunder

The man and woman in the background are the bee-keepers. Bees were very important in the Middle Ages, for in those days there was no sugar, and honey was the only sweetener available. Every village or manor had lots of bees. You can see their straw hives in the roofed building near where the woman is standing. The bee-keepers want the bees to settle, so that they can be put into a new hive. So they are banging with sticks on an iron pan. They think the bees will believe that it is thunder and so will settle down before the rain begins! Bees don't like to fly in the rain.

The men in the foreground are planting and laying a hedge. They will slash halfway through the growing bushes just above ground, bend them over and weave them around stakes. The branches continue to grow and sprout, and that makes a very good fence indeed.

A Poor Man's Farm

Here is another medieval farm. It is in Saxony, Germany, and it is a peasant farm rather than a rich manor as shown in the previous picture. The farmer is not so well dressed, and he does not possess so many farm animals. The building in the background is his house, but his farm animals live there as well. They will occupy one end of the building, while he and his family live in the other end. Above the living quarters is a loft, where hay is stored for the cattle. Perhaps the round hole is the entrance to a pigeon loft.

The Farmer's Tools

This farmer has a plough, no doubt made by the village blacksmith. The harrow is rectangular not triangular, as in the previous picture, but is made on the same principle. In the picture it is turned upside-down, to show the spikes. The sickle or reap-hook is used for cutting corn, as in the first picture; the scythe is used for mowing grass for hay. In his right hand the farmer holds a hand-rake, which can be used both for raking hay or straw and for covering newly-sown seed. His left hand holds a spade, but a spade of a special kind. It can also be called a trenching-tool, for it is used especially for digging or cleaning out trenches and drains. The pond in the right-hand corner shows that this farm is on wet soil which probably needs draining.

The farmer has two carts, one with sides made of hurdle or wickerwork, and one with board sides. The one on the left is the lighter of the two and may be pulled by hand rather than by animals. As this is a poor man's farm there are no horses; the land work is done by oxen. Nor are there any sheep. The two pigs are small, lean animals. The farmer turns them loose in the forest, to get their own living. They eat acorns and dig in the ground for roots.

Because he lives in a wet countryside the farmer is able to keep ducks, which are swimming on the pond, and also geese. It is rather surprising, too, to see a peacock perched on one of the carts. However, peacocks were much commoner on medieval farms than they are today. The young birds were kept in coops, for fattening. People also ate swans and herons then.

Guarding the Farm

The big dog is a guard dog. He prowls around the farm at night, frightening off intruders and protecting the farm animals. In the forest in the background wolves and bears still live. There may also be lynxes and wild cats, ready to prey on little pigs, calves and poultry. So the farmer needs a strong, fierce dog.

Shearing the Flock

In this medieval scene, shepherds are cutting off sheep's wool with shears. The art of shearing is to cut off all the wool in one piece, called a fleece.

To shear the sheep the shepherds are using shears. Some shepherds still do, though most now use clippers driven by electricity or by a diesel engine. One of the sheep grazing in the background has already been shorn. The others still have their woolly coats and are waiting for their turn. They do not mind at all, for the weather is warm. Shearing takes place in May or June, when the sheep have no need of the winter fleece.

Who is the old man at the right of the picture? Is he an old shepherd who has grown too old for work? If so, perhaps he carries some ointment in that pouch at his side, to put on any wounds that the shearers make when their shears slip. Or is he the farmer, come to see that the men are doing their work properly?

The farm buildings in the background are large and well built. They evidently belong to a wealthy lord, who can afford to protect the deer which are grazing quietly under the trees. The scene looks as though it is all part of a park.

Wool for Export

In the Middle Ages wool became very important. In the towns of Belgium and The Netherlands cloth-making factories were set up. Their own countries could not produce enough wool, so they bought enormous quantities from other countries in Europe, especially England. Merchants used to travel all over the country, buying wool from the farms. They became very rich and used some of their money to build lovely stone houses, churches and halls. Many of these buildings are still standing and attract thousands of tourists.

Wool, not Corn

The prices the merchants paid for wool were so high that farmers preferred to keep sheep rather than to grow corn. In many places they stopped using the plough and let grass grow in the fields instead, for the sheep to graze. In the picture there is no ploughed land at all – just grass. The monasteries, one of which is shown in our next picture, were great sheep farmers. Some of them owned tens of thousands of sheep. In those days, however, most of the sheep were quite small and their fleeces were light.

The shepherd became an important man. In the picture the men doing the shearing are under-shepherds. The head shepherd will be in the barn, supervising the packing of the fleeces. Or perhaps the well-dressed man who is looking on is the head shepherd.

Monasteries

The two monks who are ploughing live in the big buildings in the background. This is a monastery. The biggest building of all, with a little spire on one end of the roof, is the monastery's church. In front of it is a big barn, with storage space for the corn and stalls for the oxen. The rooms where the monks live, and the dining room, are in one of the other buildings in the background.

We know these are monks because of their long garments, fastened by a belt, and because of the way their hair is cut. The tops of their heads are shaved, and the hair is allowed to grow in a fringe around it. The man on the right, who has a stick to encourage the oxen, has pulled his hood over his head, so we cannot see his tonsure, as this hair style is called.

Seeking a Better Life

About fifteen hundred years ago, when the Roman Empire was breaking up, life for ordinary people became so difficult that many of them were in despair. Thinking that things would never be any better, they left their homes and wandered away into forests and deserts to become hermits. After a time there were so many of them that some of them decided to live together in groups. They lived according to strict rules, eating only plain food and wearing only rough clothes. They divided the day into three parts, one for prayer and meditation, one for eating and sleeping, and one for work.

Early Technology

Although they always settled in the wildest and loneliest places, they worked so hard and were so well organised that in time they turned their settlements into flourishing farms, such as this one. In the valley, beyond the field which is being ploughed, are gardens, neatly laid out in squares. Here the monks are growing vegetables such as cabbages, parsnips, carrots, onions and peas. Along the edges of the garden plots are rows of herbs, used not only for flavouring food but for medicines. The trees neatly spaced in the background are probably fruit trees, such as apple, pear, cherry, plum, walnut or chestnut.

The buildings are built of stone and are large and strong. Although the plough is home-made, it is well designed. It has two wheels, and there are devices for adjusting the depth of the furrow. The oxen are well fed and docile. Their wooden collars are well padded, so that the oxen will not get sores on their shoulders through pulling the plough through the heavy earth. The monk in the background is sowing seed, by hand, on land that has already been ploughed.

Serving his Lordship

What a contrast we have in this picture of the early seventeenth century! In the foreground and to the left we see England much as it was in medieval times. In the top right-hand corner stands a magnificent new country house, recently built by some rich lord. It is in a new Italian style, known as Palladian, which came into fashion about this time. In front of it are formal gardens, laid out to a geometrical design. The wide path down to the river is dead straight, and the standard rose-bushes are all equally spaced. The man and lady strolling down the path are dressed in rich clothes, so long and so tightly buttoned that it would be impossible for the wearers to do any work.

Windmill and Watermill

Upstream, near the mill, is a barge propelled by a sail. Most likely it is carrying corn to the mill, which is worked by means of a great water-wheel. The mill harnesses the powerful flow of the water to turn one great stone upon another, grinding and crushing the corn between them. A village or small town lies in the valley beyond the mill. We can see the church, with a spire, and some of the houses. On the crest of the hill beyond is a windmill.

On the near side of the river several farming activities are going on. In the foreground cows are being milked in a field. This was common practice until quite recent times, though now they are tied in stalls in milking parlours.

In the field behind the pasture, men are busy harvesting corn. One man is cutting the standing corn with a sickle. Another, on the far side of the field, is gathering up the fallen stalks and tying them into sheaves. Over much of the field sheaves are stood upright, to dry. One man is carrying a sheaf on the prong on his shoulder. He is following a cartload of sheaves which has just passed over the bridge. This cart is drawn by two small horses, one in trace harness in front of the other.

Cider

Approaching the bridge from the far side is a man on horseback. The horse also carries panniers, or baskets, of goods slung on either side of its back. He has just passed sheep grazing in a meadow. On the other side of the hedge a man is lifting to his lips a wooden bottle of cider, a drink made from apples.

Beyond the gate we can see the house where the cider is made. The man coming out of the doorway is talking to another who is working the cider press, which squeezes the juice out of the apples. By the door are two large barrels, either full of cider or waiting to be filled.

Harvesting Fruit

This is a picture of fruit harvesting in Holland in the seventeenth century. The season is autumn, and the fruits being harvested are apples and grapes. The weather is fine, so the fruit-pickers are trying to get all the fruits harvested before the autumn storms begin.

Men are using ladders to reach the apples high in the trees. Women are picking up the apples which have fallen to the ground. Some of the grape-vines are trained along wooden frames and look like hedges. The man sitting at a table near the top of the picture is beneath the shade of a grape-vine trained to a trellis.

Baskets and Panniers

The fruit-pickers are using several sorts of baskets. Those in the trees have large handles which can be hung from branches by a crook. When they are lowered to the ground the apples are poured into deep, bucket-shaped hampers or panniers. These fit neatly on either side of the backs of donkeys. Donkeys are evidently the chief beasts of burden in this part of the country. The grapes, which are being gathered by women on the path in the middle of the picture, are carried in flat baskets, though later they are transferred to deeper ones.

The big circular building in the top right-hand corner is apparently a ruined castle. Only the lower part of the tower remains and this has been made into an inn. The man sitting at the table under the vine is enjoying a drink of wine or cider, watched by the innkeeper's wife. The man striding away with a greyhound gambolling around his feet is carrying, from a pole over his shoulder, a basket of grapes and two leather bottles of wine. The man facing him is evidently inviting his wife or girl-friend to come up to the inn for a drink.

Barrel-making

In the foreground there are a number of upright barrels, into which apples are being packed. Instead of being made into cider, these apples are going to market, in one of the Dutch towns. The man with the raised hammer is sealing one of the barrels. Another man is fitting iron hoops around a barrel, to keep it from bursting open. We can see a pile of hoops on the ground, waiting to be used. Two children have borrowed two of them, to play with. Men who make barrels are called coopers, and theirs is a very skilled trade. Anyone whose name is Cooper today probably has an ancestor who made barrels.

This is a cheerful scene. Everyone seems busy and happy. Even the donkey in the foreground is calling cheerfully to its mates.

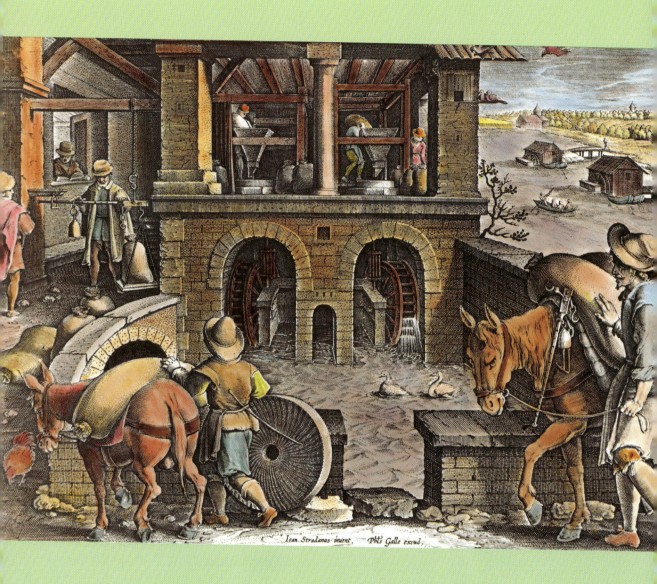

Bringing Corn to the Mill

This picture shows a seventeenth-century water-mill at work. Farmers are bringing in their grain, in large sacks slung across the backs of donkeys or horses, to be ground into flour. The grain is crushed between two great stone wheels, like the spare one shown leaning against a wall in the foreground. The grooves with which the stone is patterned allow the flour to escape.

On the left of the picture one of the millers is weighing a sack of corn, which has just arrived for grinding. The weighing device is known as a steel-yard, which was still being occasionally used not many years ago. Through the window we can see a clerk, seated at a desk and entering the weights in a ledger.

Crushing Corn into Flour

When they have been weighed the sacks of grain are taken into the upper room and emptied into the funnel-like containers, which are known as hoppers. From them the grain pours down on the stones in the grinding chamber. The water wheels supply the power which turns the massive grinding-stones, crushing the corn into flour.

Although they were so necessary, mills were not popular with farmers. For many hundreds of years farmers and cottagers ground their corn at home, or rather, their wives or servants did the grinding. The tool they used was the quern, which consisted of two flat, round stones between which the grain was crushed. The upper one had a handle to turn it and a hole in the middle into which the grain was poured.

Damming a river and building a mill was quite an expensive process and was usually carried out by the local landowner, the lord of the manor. Having gone to such trouble and expense, he naturally wanted to get back as much money as possible, so he usually insisted that all the people living on his manor should bring their grain to his mill for grinding. Then he kept back some of the flour to pay for the work. The farmers and villagers were angry at having to pay for something which had formerly cost them nothing.

Later, when mills were owned by the millers who operated them, the farmers still grumbled. They complained that the miller kept back more than his fair share of the flour. Here is a comment which later became a schoolboy rhyme:

Miller-dee, miller-dee,
  dusty poll,
How many sacks of flour
  hast thou stole?
In goes a bushel,
  out comes a peck.
Hang old miller-dee up
  by the neck!

A Busy Farmyard

In this farmyard scene of the eighteenth century, you will see that the house windows have glass in them, though the panes are small. Glass was becoming more common though still expensive. The dairy at the end of the house, however, has upright bars and no glass. That is because dairies had to be kept cool and well ventilated. The timber frames of the house are picturesque, but that is not why the house is built that way. In former times the house would have been built entirely of wood, but trees are not as plentiful as they used to be. So the timber is used only for the framework, and the intervening panels are filled in with hurdlework and plaster or with a mixture of hardened clay or chalk.

Haymaking in Summer

It is summer, and haymaking is in progress. The ricks in the district are round, for we can see two of them, already thatched to keep out the rain, in the background on the right. The hay is for feeding the cows in winter, but note that all the animals are being fed on grain or meal now. There is meal in the trough where the pigs are feeding. A girl is scattering grains of corn for the chicken to pick up. A man is feeding ducks and geese on the pond. In earlier centuries most of the grain and meal would have been needed for people to eat; there would have been very little left over for animals.

Pigs from China

The pigs are very much better animals than those we have seen in previous pictures. About this time pigs of a better type began to arrive in Europe from China. They were crossed with local pigs to produce the nice, fat, rounded animals shown. The dogs, too, are smaller and more friendly than the great fierce hounds that guarded the farmyard from wolves and robbers in earlier times. The dog sitting outside the kennel looks like a bull terrier. The cows are still milked outdoors, however, by a milkmaid. Water still has to be drawn from a well by a windlass. The farmer's wife does not buy wool for making clothes from a shop but spins the wool from the farm's sheep. It is quite a pleasant task, sitting outside the farmhouse door on a summer day.

The cone-shaped cage by the well is a hen-coop. Inside it is a mother hen. The baby chicks can run in and out, but the bars of the cage prevent the hen from wandering away. Behind it is a bench with three bee-hives. On the wall of the shed is a gibbet, where the carcases of birds and animals thought to be vermin are nailed up. The big bird so displayed is probably a hawk.

A Swarm of Bees in May

Bee-keeping was still, in the early eighteenth century, a very important branch of farming. In earlier times every village or manor had a specialist bee-keeper known as a beeward. Some of the people in the picture would be specialists, too, but the artist has put in more persons than would have been employed in any bee-garden.

Honey and Wax

Bees were kept to provide honey and wax. Before sugar became readily available, honey was the only sweetening substance that most people ever tasted. It was also much in demand for making an alcoholic drink called mead.

Beeswax was used for making candles as well as for polishing furniture. Candles of beeswax were important features in the services of the Roman Catholic church, to which in the Middle Ages almost everyone belonged, and vast numbers of them were needed.

In very early days people relied on wild bees, which lived in the forests around every village. The bees made nests in hollow trees, and so honey-gatherers used to hang hollow logs in trees, in the hope that the bees would use them. They often did. Then someone invented straw bee-hives, or skeps, like those in the picture. The frame is made of peeled brambles or willow wands, with straw woven around it. In the foreground, however, an up-to-date beekeeper is studying a hive consisting of rectangular frames set side by side in a wooden box, like modern bee-hives.

Bees Killed in Autumn

When skeps were used the beekeeper killed off in autumn all the bees from the hives from which he took the honey. He retained just enough hives to start again next spring. He hoped that then the bees would form new swarms in early summer, to make a surplus of honey again for the autumn. An old rhyme says,

> A swarm of bees in May,
> is worth a load of hay;
> A swarm of bees in June,
> is worth a silver spoon;
> A swarm of bees in July,
> isn't worth a fly.

In this picture the bees are swarming. New queen bees have been hatched and are flying off, with crowds of worker bees, to form new colonies.

In the forest in the background some swarms have settled in trees and people are collecting them. Some men are shaking trees, to dislodge the bees.

In the bee garden a man and two women are trying to persuade another swarm to settle down rather than fly away. As in the picture on page 12 they are trying to imitate thunder.

Jethro Tull

The man in the centre of this picture is Jethro Tull. The implement he is using is a seed-drill, which he has just invented. The neighbours, who have come to see it, do not approve. Some are laughing at it. Others shake their heads in disapproval because it is different from anything they have been used to.

Sowing Seeds in Rows

The seed drill is a new method of sowing seeds. As previous pictures have shown us, the old method was to scatter the seeds by hand over the ploughed fields and then to cover them with soil by using a rake or a harrow. In the background on the right we can see men sowing seed in this old-fashioned way. Another man with a horse-drawn harrow is following them. Birds waiting to feed on the seed are lined up on the stone wall. Others are flying around, and others are actually feeding around the feet of the sowers. They pay no attention to the numerous scarecrows. An old farming rhyme used to say that a farmer should sow four times as many seeds as were really necessary:

> One for the sparrow,
> One for the crow,
> One to rot,
> And one to grow.

Jethro Tull, who was born in 1674, was also looking for a method of sowing seeds so that the crop could be kept free from weeds while it was growing. He invented another implement called a horse-hoe, which consisted of iron blades for uprooting weeds, set in a frame and pulled by a horse. But to use it, the seeds had to be sown in rows, so that the blades could run between them without disturbing the seed. The only way Tull could at first think of for sowing seeds in rows was to set them by hand, one by one.

On Sundays Jethro Tull liked to play the church organ. One Sunday, when he was doing so, the answer to his problem suddenly came to him. He would make an implement based on the organ pipes. The seed would be poured into funnel-shaped containers from which it would descend through pipes, into the soil.

Hoeing by Horsepower

In the picture we can see the implement he made. It is constructed of light wood and is mounted on large wheels, so that one horse can pull it easily. The front box carries a store of seed, so that when the containers (or hoppers) are empty they can be re-filled from the box. Although people laughed at and opposed Tull, his seed-drill was a great invention. Most seeds are still sown by similar drills, though they have been vastly improved since his day.

The First Agricultural Show

Although the title of this picture is 'The Woburn Sheep-Shearing', there seems to be only a little sheep-shearing going on. Two sheep in the right-hand corner are actually being shorn, while nearby a shepherd is selecting another one for shearing. One of the sheep in the foreground has been shorn, but all the others still have their fleeces.

Mostly the people are standing about, talking and looking at farm animals. Only a few of them are shepherds; we can see one in the foreground, wearing a smock and carrying a shepherd's long-handled crook. Most of them are gentlemen, stylishly dressed in top-hats and tailed coats. The man on horseback in the centre is the Duke of Bedford, who owns the estate. The notice on the big barn states it was he who erected it.

Occupation for Gentlemen

In our previous pictures most of the people shown are busy doing some sort of farm work, and they are dressed in their working-clothes. In the first picture of all, some of the men do not even have boots or shoes. What has happened is that by this date, 1804, farming has started to become an occupation of gentlemen. They have large farms on which they like to grow heavy crops of grain, and particularly they like to own handsome farm animals, which they can show off to their friends.

About the middle of the eighteenth century Viscount Townshend, a Norfolk landowner, started farming his land by what has become known as the Norfolk four-course husbandry. Each field of his farm grew, in successive years, turnips, barley or oats, clover and rye-grass, and – in the fourth year – wheat. The turnips and the clover and rye-grass were eaten by sheep, penned on them so that their dung greatly enriched the soil. A little later his example was followed by his neighbour, Thomas Coke.

Four-course Husbandry

The new system proved so successful that farmers came from all over England to inspect it. So Coke decided to invite them to come to one big event, his sheep-shearings. In one year more than 7,000 people came. They spent the day inspecting his crops and farm animals, and in the evenings after supper they talked about the new methods.

After a time other landowners organised similar events. Our picture shows a sheep-shearing on the Duke of Bedford's farm at Woburn. Some of the visitors are watching the sheep-shearing, but many others are looking at the fine cattle and prize-winning sheep. In later years these events developed into the present-day agricultural shows.

The Beginning of Automation

For hundreds of years grain was threshed by men with flails. At harvest-time the corn, cut by reap-hook or scythe, was tied into sheaves, and the sheaves were either made into ricks or stored in barns. In winter they were taken out of store, laid on a threshing-floor in a barn and had the grain beaten out of them by flails.

Threshing Machines

Soon after steam-engines had been invented, farmers started using them to drive threshing-machines. At first these were stationary engines, which stood in the farmyard and were connected by a broad leather belt with the threshing-machine which stood in the barn. It did not take long, however, for manufacturers to develop a portable threshing-machine, like the one in the picture.

The actual threshing apparatus is inside the box-on-wheels. It consists of a set of iron beaters attached to a spindle and made to revolve very fast by means of a series of pulleys connected with the steam-engine. The men on the box are cutting the bonds of sheaves and feeding the corn gently into the machine. There are protective boards to prevent them slipping and injuring themselves on the rapidly-spinning beaters. The men in the right foreground are passing the sheaves from the rick, which is rapidly shrinking, to the men on the box. The men in the background are building a new rick of the straw, which the machine discards at its farther end.

This is a very early type of threshing-machine. The grain is being deposited by the machine on a cloth spread on the ground. The farmer is watching and trying to estimate how much there is. Later models allowed the grain to be poured direct into sacks. The driver has nothing to do with the threshing. His job is to drive the engine. The cylinder, or boiler, is filled with water, and he shovels coal, as required, into the furnace at the back, near where he is standing. When the threshing is finished he will reverse the engine, hitch the box to the rear of it, and set off for the next farm. The outfit trundled along the country lanes at about two or three miles an hour!

Machine Wreckers

When threshing-machines were first introduced they were the cause of riots in the countryside. Farm workers were afraid that the machines would do all the threshing and so deprive them of a job in winter. So they went around smashing and burning the machines. But the threshing-machines had come to stay and were in common use until the 1940s. As we can see, they did provide work for quite a lot of men.

McCormick's Reaper

When we think of the Industrial Revolution, when men began inventing all sorts of machines to do jobs which had previously been done by hand, we usually think of factories and smoky towns. But inventors were soon thinking of ideas to make farm work easier and quicker too.

One of the most important jobs on a farm is the gathering of the harvest. For hundreds of years the corn had been cut by men with scythes or sickles, which was either a very slow operation or else required many men to do it. Anything that could be done to speed it up would be valuable, for rain at harvest-time was frequent and often spoiled much corn.

Scissoring the Corn

Although many inventors studied the problem, they could not, for a long time, find the answer. What they were considering were ways of making a super or mechanical scythe or sickle, which would cut the standing corn by sweeping or chopping, and nothing they tried seemed to work. It wasn't until they thought of how scissors worked that they made progress.

The mechanical reaper worked just like scissors. A steel rod on which triangular blades were mounted was made to move very rapidly backwards and forwards against a similar series of stationary teeth. Both the moving blades and the stationary one had sharp edges which fitted closely together, so that anything they encountered was quickly mown down. The first model to come into general use was a reaper developed in America by Cyrus McCormick.

Two Men and two Horses

The one in the picture is drawn by two horses, but it is working on level ground, and on a hill slope it might need an extra horse. The cutting blades are fitted horizontally two or three inches above the ground. The beaters which revolve just in front of the knives press the standing corn towards them, thus making it easier for them to cut it. The arm of the machine which looks like a comb is a device to make the severed corn-stalks lie flat and to deposit them on the ground well away from the machine. In the foreground a man is gathering them up and tying them into sheaves. It was not long, however, before the reaping-machine was improved by adding to it a device for tying sheaves. It was then called a self-binding reaper, or, as it became commonly known, a binder. It was in common use until about thirty years ago, and some are still used today. We can see how economical it was. In this harvest field there are only two men in sight.

A Farmhouse Dairy

In an earlier picture we saw, at the end of a farmhouse, a room labelled 'Dairy'. Here we see the inside of a farmhouse dairy, though of a rather later date. The picture was drawn about 1860.

The type of churn which the dairymaid is turning is a barrel churn, which came into use about the beginning of the nineteenth century. Before that, churns of plunger type were used. We can see one just to the right of the barrel churn, half-hidden by the tank. It looks something like a giant salt-cellar.

The handle sticking out at the top is connected to a circular disc at the bottom. After the cream had been poured in, the dairymaid had to keep lifting the disc up and down, by means of the handle, until the cream turned into butter. It was very hard work and took a long time. Churning with a barrel churn was not much quicker but was not quite so hard. On the floor, in line with the doorway, is another type of churn, with a side cut away to show how it works. The handle is connected to a set of paddles which

vigorously stir the cream. This is for making a smaller quantity of butter. It would have to be placed on a table before the handle could be turned.

Also on the floor, in the foreground, are a number of shallow pans. These are for extracting the cream from milk. The milk is poured into them and allowed to stand overnight. By morning the cream will have risen to the top, like a crust. It can then be skimmed off.

In this dairy both butter and cheese are made. For cheese-making the milk is poured into the metal tank on the right. A substance called rennet is added, to make it curdle. In time the liquid milk becomes mostly solid, just as when we leave a bottle of milk on the doorstep all day in the summer sun. The remaining liquid is then drained off. For the next few hours the curd, as it is called, is chopped into small pieces, drained again, salted, turned by hand several times and generally worked over until every drop of liquid has been squeezed out and a big lump of semi-solid stuff is left behind. This is put into moulds and pressed. In the background, near the door, we can see a cheese press, with three cheeses in it. The essential part is the screw above the cheeses, which can be tightened to increase the pressure. To the left of the doorway is a smaller press, for making one very large cheese.

The Autumn Round-up

When Europeans began to settle in North America they found the eastern part of the continent, where they settled first, very like the Europe from which they had sailed. The climate was similar, though rather colder in winter. There were forests and meadows, mountains and streams. When they penetrated farther west, though, they found vast plains (prairies), rivers broader and longer than they had ever seen in Europe, and – beyond them – huge areas of wild, barren country in the foothills of high mountain ranges.

In the east they could make fields and farms, grow crops, and keep cattle, pigs, sheep and poultry, just as they had in Europe. Farther west it was much more difficult. They found that the best way to make use of the land was to ranch it – that means, to turn cattle loose to get their living as best they could on the sparse herbage. As there was so little grass, the ranches had to be very large, sometimes tens of thousands or even hundreds of thousands of acres. The cattle roamed freely over these immense areas, almost like wild animals.

Branding

They were not really wild, though. They all had owners, who paid cowboys to keep an eye on them. Every autumn the cowboys rounded up the cattle and branded, with their owner's mark, all the calves that had been born that year. At certain times, too, they collected the mature cattle and sent off the surplus ones to market. Most of the beef eaten in American cities came from cattle born and reared on the ranches, and much of it still does.

In the picture three cowboys are rounding up a steer. It is a big, adult steer, fit to go to market, and it has already been branded as a calf. We can see the brand mark on its side. The cowboys are going to catch the animal by means of a lasso, which they will throw expertly over its head or its horns.

Bison

When Europeans first came to America they found enormous herds of bison grazing on the plains and on the mountain pastures. After they had nearly exterminated them by hunting them for meat, or merely for the pleasure of hunting, they brought in European cattle to replace them. Many of these cattle had wandered northwards from the Spanish settlements in Mexico, but as the country became more thickly populated the ranchers introduced English bulls to improve the breed. Crossbreds based on the white-faced Hereford breed are now the most common type to be seen on the ranches of America.

Cotton Plantations

Although parts of North America are very like northern Europe, other parts of the continent are much warmer. The southern states of the United States are in the same latitude as Egypt and northern India, and have a similar climate. So the farmers there grow different crops from those farther north.

One of these crops is cotton, a plant which originally came from India. It is cultivated for its fibres, which are woven into cloth. It needs plenty of rain during its long growing season, and then a period of hot, dry weather when the seeds are ripening on the plant. The southern states of America, especially those in and around the lower valley of the river Mississippi, have just the right climate, so vast quantities of cotton are grown there.

Cotton is a low, bushy plant. The fibres for which it is grown are a fuzzy mass, attached to the seeds, called lint. The seeds are contained in a capsule known as a boll, up to eleven seeds in each boll. When they are ripe, the boll splits open, revealing the white fluffy lint, which is then ready for picking.

Cotton picking is a long process, for the bolls do not all ripen at the same

time. The pickers have to go over the same plants time after time. When cotton-growing began in America everybody in the family used to go into the fields to help with the cotton picking. Soon, however, the bigger farms began to employ slave labour, the slaves being chiefly negroes fetched from Africa, though some were European convicts. Now in American much of the picking is done by machine, though in some other countries the cotton is still harvested by hand.

In the picture the cotton harvest is in full swing. Negro slaves are picking the cotton into wicker baskets. When full, these are taken to a waiting wagon, one of which can be seen on the far side of the field. The wagon takes its load to the cotton gin, which is a machine something like the threshing-machine shown on an English farm on page 34. Its purpose is to break open the cotton bolls and extract the fibre (or lint). The cotton gin is housed in one of the tiled buildings in the background.

The extracted cotton is then packed in bales, some samples of which can be seen on the mule-drawn wagon in the foreground. The two chimneys smoking in the distance are the funnels of a paddle steamer on the river Mississippi. The boat is waiting to be loaded with cotton, to take to the factories in the big industrial cities in the northern States. Note the dog, seeking the shade of the wagon; it is very hot in the cotton fields in summer.

The Agricultural Union

In early times, when everybody worked on the land, there were no farm workers working for wages. Villagers in those days had no need of money, for there were no shops where they could spend it. When they had to pay taxes, rents, tithes and other debts they did so by working for a time for the man to whom the payments were due.

Farming for Wages

Later, when people became used to trading in cash rather than services, many villagers who had only small farms used to increase their income by working at times for their larger neighbours. In time some of them sold their few fields to the bigger farmers and so became dependent on their wages.

By the early nineteenth century farm workers were finding life very hard. The British were fighting a war against the French under Napoleon, and this caused the price of food to rise so high that many of the workers couldn't afford to buy it. So their wages had to be supplemented by a subsidy. When the war was over wages were still kept very low, because the farmers said that the workers were getting a subsidy anyway.

At last the farm workers decided to form a union. Their leader was Joseph Arch, who campaigned for a union through the middle years of the nineteenth century. Eventually he succeeded in founding an Agricultural Workers' Union in 1872.

In the picture he is addressing a meeting at Wellesbourne, near his home in Warwickshire. In the corners of the poster are four scenes illustrating ways in which the Union was able to help its members. In one scene a man who has been thatching a house is seen falling off a ladder. In those days there was no national insurance, but the Union provided insurance against accidents. The Union member was also insured against sickness, which in former times had been impossible. When he died, the Union saw that he was decently buried.

To a New Life

In the bottom right-hand picture we see a family of farm workers emigrating. Now that the farms were much larger than once they were and much of the farm work was being done by machines, many farm workers were finding themselves unemployed. Some went to work in the new industrial towns, but others emigrated. The Union helped them with their fares to overseas countries such as Canada, the United States, Australia and New Zealand. There many of them created new farms out of the wilderness and became prosperous farmers, greatly increasing the food supply of the world.

London's Meat Market

This busy scene shows London's Smithfield Market about 150 years ago.

By the time this picture was drawn the market was dealing only in cattle and sheep. The sheep are confined in square pens of hurdles, while the cattle are tied to rails or are being led by men with ropes. Some of the cattle have escaped and are being chased by men and dogs. A white one in the right foreground has lowered its head and is attempting to fight. There must be hundreds and hundreds of animals in the market. We can imagine the noise that is going on.

Although Smithfield was once an open field, we can see that the town has grown around it. There are streets and tall buildings in every direction. We may wonder how the animals got to the market, in an age when there were no lorries or even railways. The answer is that they walked.

As London grew larger and larger and its inhabitants became richer it needed enormous supplies of food. It needed much more than the farms just outside its limits could supply, so eventually some of it came from long distances.

The drovers stopped at the same farms overnight. The farmers would expect them and would set aside a field for the animals to rest in. They would also provide food for them, for which the drovers would pay. A shoemaker in Somerset used to make little shoes of soft leather for footsore geese passing through his village!

In the picture buyers and sellers are discussing prices with each other. Later in the nineteenth century the animals were sold by auction. The buyers paid in golden guineas. Often the drovers had to carry thousands of pounds in gold right across England, to pay the farmers who had sent the livestock. Drovers had to be very honest men.

Cattle walked to London all the way from Wales and Scotland. Sheep came from Dorset, Gloucestershire and Wales. Turkeys from Norfolk. Geese from Devon. Even the geese and turkeys walked.

They were brought in huge flocks and herds by men known as drovers. In those days much of England was open, unfenced country, so the animals could walk quietly along, feeding as they went. Cattle would travel fifteen or more miles a day; other animals less. The drovers followed regular routes known as droveways, skirting the smaller towns. Now that those towns have grown you will often find a Droveway or Drove Road not far from the centre.

Beer – the Poor Man's Drink

From very early times people made alcoholic drinks. Almost the only alternative was water, and too often the water supplies were polluted. Tea was imported in the eighteenth century but was for a long time so expensive that only rich people could afford to drink it. Most farms, and many cottages as well, brewed their own beer, except in the apple-growing districts of the west where they made cider instead.

Home-brewing

Brewing is a rather complicated process, and the picture makes it look simpler than it really is. The man on the left is turning the handle of a grinding-machine. He is grinding malt, which is barley that has germinated. Many farms had their own malthouses, where barley was spread out on the floor of a hot, damp room until it started to sprout.

The ground malt was put into a round, shallow tub like the one in the middle of the picture. Here it was mixed with hot water. The man doing the brewing is stirring it with a long wooden ladle known as a mash oar. After it had been thoroughly mixed and allowed to stand for four hours it was poured into the copper and had some hops added to it. It was then boiled for four hours. The woman in the picture is stoking the fire to keep the copper boiling. When it was drawn off it had to pass through a wickerwork filter, which a man is holding. It went into another brewing tub and was allowed to stand overnight, with yeast added to cause it to ferment. Steam is rising from a brewing tub behind the casks.

In the morning the yeast was skimmed off and the beer ladled into the casks, which stand on the right of the picture. We can also see a sieve (for straining the beer, so that no hop seeds or other particles should be left in it), a supply of firewood, and several stools and wooden buckets. On the stool in front of the casks is a candle in a candlestick with a long handle. This was for putting in the casks before they were used, to make sure that they were not filled with stagnant air. If the air was foul, the candle went out.

Cider

Cider-making was much less complicated. The apples had simply to be crushed. In the picture this is being done between the great stones of a cider-mill, turned by a horse which walks in circles round it. The pulp left after the grinding was put through a cider-press, which was very like the cheese-press shown in a previous picture. The juice squeezed out was poured into casks and allowed to ferment.

Haymaking in Summer

One of the chief handicaps that farmers in England and other northern countries have is the shortness of the summers. They used to base their farming programmes on five months of summer and seven months of winter. The rule is still sound, though modern plant-breeders have developed plants which will start growing early and continue growing until late in autumn.

Winter Fodder

Grass is the crop for which the English climate is best suited. This is fortunate, because cattle and sheep can grow fat and produce a lot of milk on a diet of grass. But farmers have to solve the problem of feeding their farm animals in winter, when grass does not grow.

From very early times the most popular answer has been to make hay. The grass is allowed to grow until it is at its best. That means just as it is starting to flower, in June or July. If there is a lot of clover growing with the grass, so much the better. Clover makes excellent hay.

After the grass is cut it is allowed to lie on the ground for several days, to dry. Formerly it was cut by scythe or reap-hook; now the work is done by a tractor-mounted grasscutter. When the top surface is dry, the grass is turned over and shaken about so that the underneath stalks shall dry as well. Today the turning and shaking is done by machine, but formerly men and women worked at it with prongs and rakes. When the hay is properly 'made' it is quite dry and has a lovely, fragrant scent.

Unfortunately, June and July are often stormy months. Haymakers always keep an anxious eye on the clouds. Once the hay is dry enough to be turned, the haymakers are usually engaged in a race against time. Hayfields used to be filled with dozens of people, even small children, turning and tossing the hay as fast as they could. When at last it is dry, it has to be carted to a barn or a rick as quickly as possible. At this season, the haymakers work very long hours. They cannot start too early in the morning because the hay is often wet with dew, and this has to dry off, but they make up for it by working late in the evening.

Time for a Rest

So these haymakers are glad of a break at tea-time. The wife or daughter of one of the men has bought them bread-and-cheese and cake in a basket and hot tea in jugs. This picture was probably taken about 1910. In earlier times the men would be drinking beer. But they have a fine Shire horse, instead of a tractor, to pull their cart. The horse, of course, likes both grass and hay to eat, and in haymaking time it would get both.

51

Holidays in the Hop-fields

Hops are used in brewing beer. They improve its flavour and prevent it from fermenting too much and so going sour.

When almost every farm made its own beer, it also had its own hop-garden. Even now in many villages hop vines can still be found climbing over the hedges of gardens where they were once cultivated.

Breaking the Law

When hops were introduced, however, in the reign of Henry VIII, many people did not like the taste they gave to the beer. They preferred the old-fashioned English ale, made without hops. Laws were passed to try to stop brewers from using hops, but people soon grew to like the new flavour and so the laws were forgotten.

Most beer nowadays is made in big breweries, who buy their hops from farmers who specialize in growing them.

These farmers live in certain districts which are specially suitable for growing hops. The hop plants need a deep, rich soil and a sheltered position because they grow so tall. It is an advantage to have woodlands nearby, where long hop-poles can be cut. The districts where hops are now grown are Kent, north-western Surrey and a corner of Herefordshire and Worcestershire.

In hop-gardens the hop-plants wind their stems on to poles ten or fifteen feet high. When the hops are ready for picking, in late summer or early autumn, quite an army of pickers is needed. The poles have to be taken down and the hops stripped from them. Where small quantities were grown a farmer could recruit a team of pickers locally, but for harvesting the hops in the big fields of Kent and Surrey loads of pickers were brought out from London. Whole families used to arrive and camp out in shelters or tents. The picture shows a typical family of 'hoppers' from the East End of London in Victoria's reign. For them it was a country holiday, much looked forward to all the summer. And a very pleasant holiday it was, too, except when it rained.

Oast-houses

The frames in the picture are supports for the hop sacks. The hops are collected in wicker baskets and poured into the sacks until the sacks are full. They are then taken to the oast-houses, which are specially-built buildings with kilns for drying the hops, something like the malt-houses for drying barley, as described on a previous page.

Today the hops are picked by machines and dried in electrically-heated kilns.

Farewell to the Horse

The age of the modern farm tractor began in 1889 when an American company fitted a petrol engine to a steam tractor. In the first ten years or so of the twentieth century several factories for manufacturing tractors were set up, mostly in America. Progress became more rapid during the First World War. Henry Ford, the American manufacturer, was already busy making vans, cars and trucks for military use, so he started making tractors as well. After the war European factories, which had been making war supplies, also switched to developing tractors.

Pulling a Plough

The picture shows an early French model, made by a firm named Hansa Lloyd. It is a very primitive machine, with iron wheels. The width of the rear wheels is doubled by means of a special attachment, designed to help them to grip on wet, slippery or soft soil. The steering is controlled simply by chains fixed to the front axle. To start the engine the driver has to swing the handle at the front – a long and back-breaking job. The driver has a roof over his head but otherwise is given no protection from the weather. The two-furrowed plough at the rear is simply being hauled along by a chain. It needs a man perched on a seat at the back to steer it. The tall lever is to enable him to adjust the depth of the furrows. However, the quality of the work being done is quite good.

How great was the change that this tractor represented is shown by the fact that the other work in the field is being done not by horses but by oxen. They are breaking up the clods of earth by pulling a ring-roller over them. The soil is then ready for sowing.

Slow to Develop

American tractors were introduced into Europe in 1917, but they were not immediately adopted by every farmer. Twenty years later most of the farm work was still being done by horses. One of the problems was that machinery manufacturers did not at first make implements to fit to tractors. Farmers had to buy horse-drawn implements and adapt them. Also there was little money between the wars to spare on farms. Farmers found it cheaper to breed horses than to buy tractors.

Tractors did not necessarily do farm work better than horses. They simply did it more quickly. So when, as the Second World War approached, many more fields had to be ploughed and cultivated, the demand for tractors increased. By that time, too, tractors had been greatly improved. For one thing, they had pneumatic tyres.

Farming Becomes Mechanized

Farming is now almost fully mechanized. The picture shows neat little Massey-Ferguson tractors, very different from the clumsy, unwieldy one of seventy years ago. They all have pneumatic tyres, and the driver sits in a comfortable cab, usually with heating and often with air conditioning and even a radio.

Every Job on the Farm

More important, the range of implements made for use with tractors now covers almost every job on the farm. It includes ploughs, cultivators, mowing-machines, rotary cultivators, balers, post-hole diggers, hedge-cutters, draining tools, pumps, drills, spraying equipment and harvesters for many special crops. One of the most important developments was that of the power-take-off. This allows the power produced by the tractor's engine to be transmitted to the implement being used.

The picture shows tractors operating one of the most modern farming devices. They are collecting straw, which has been left lying in the harvest field after a combine-harvester has done its work. The straw will be useful for bedding for cattle and pigs during the winter, and, in any case, it has to be moved before the field can be used for another crop. The implement being used by the tractor in the foreground is a big-baler. It gathers the straw and rolls it tightly into a giant bale, like a huge swiss roll. The advantages of making a bale of this shape and size is that only the outer layers of straw get wet.

However, the bales have to be moved. If we look closely at the surface of the field in the foreground we shall see lines of green shoots. These are young grass plants. The seed was sown at the same time as the corn, in spring, and now that the corn has been removed it is starting to grow quickly. Soon it will cover the ground, but not if it is smothered by straw and bales. Unfortunately, each of those bales weighs half a ton! To handle them the farthest tractor is equipped with an automatic lifting device. Using its own power it easily lifts a bale and places it gently on the low trailer drawn by the third tractor.

A Self-propelled Factory

The combine-harvester which cut and threshed the corn is no longer tractor-drawn. Like many other of the larger farm machines, it is self-propelled.

However mechanized farming may become in the future, we may be sure it will never change its nature. It will still be tied to the seasons and to the age-old tasks of preparing the ground, sowing the seed, and reaping the harvest.

Acknowledgements and Sources of Pictures

cover A mural of Jethro Tull and his seed drill, painted in the 1950s and in the Science Museum, London. (The Science Museum)

page 10 Three drawings from an eleventh-century calendar of the agricultural year. The calendar is part of a manuscript, which was hand-written and illustrated by monks. (Peter Newark's Historical Pictures)

page 12 An illustration from a fourteenth- or fifteenth-century manuscript showing the largely self-supporting way of life on a medieval manor. (Fotomas Index)

page 14 An engraving from *Strutt's Chronicles* (1777), showing what a Saxon farmyard probably looked like. (Mary Evans Picture Library)

page 16 A painting, probably a miniature, illustrating the month of June in a medieval manuscript of the sixteenth century. (Wayland Picture Library).

page 18 An engraving, probably from a book or periodical, made in Germany in the nineteenth century, showing what a monastery farm in the fifteenth or sixteenth century would have looked like. (Mary Evans Picture Library)

page 20 A seventeeth-century engraving, very likely from a book on husbandry. (Fotomas Index)

page 22 A Dutch engraving from a calendar, showing the months September and October. Probably seventeenth century. (Fotomas Index)

page 24 A sixteenth-century, highly detailed engraving, probably a book illustration. (The Mansell Collection)

page 26 Late eighteenth-century print of a farmyard, probably made to illustrate a book on agriculture. (BBC Hulton Picture Library)

page 28 An illustration to a French work, *Le Nouveau Theatre d'Agriculture et menage des champs* by Le Sieur Liger published in 1723. This was a study of new methods of agriculture and farming. (BBC Hulton Picture Library)

page 30 This is the picture which appears on the cover.

page 32 An engraving by J. C. Stadtler and T. Morris done in 1811 after the painting *Woburn Sheepshearing* in 1804 and dedicated to the Duke of Bedford. (BBC Hulton Picture Library)

page 34 An engraving which appeared in the *Illustrated London News* periodical of 19th June, 1851. (Wayland Picture Library)

page 36 A coloured engraving made in the mid-nineteenth century, probably reproduced in a journal or book on agriculture. (Ann Ronan Picture Library)

page 38–9 An illustration from *Practical Farming* by R. D. Pringle published in Britain in 1860. (John Topham Picture Library)

page 40 A nineteenth-century painting by the American artist, Charles M. Russell. (Peter Newark's Western Americana)

page 42–3 A print by the nineteenth-century American printmakers, Currier and Ives, who specialized in portraying the American way of life. (The Mansell Collection)

page 44 Part of a coloured engraving, made in Britain in the late nineteenth century, almost certainly as an illustration to a periodical. (Museum of English Rural Life, University of Reading.

page 46–7 A very detailed nineteenth-century coloured engraving, which may have been commissioned to illustrate a book. (Fotomas Index)

page 48 Drawings by Thomas Pyne from his *Microcosm*, published early in the nineteenth century. (Fotomas Index)

page 50 'Bait time', a photograph taken early in the twentieth century during harvest. 'Bait' is an old-fashioned dialect word for a snack. (John Topham Picture Library)

page 52 'East Kent Hop Gardens', an Edwardian photograph probably taken by local photographers. (John Topham Picture Library)

page 54 A photograph taken in France in 1920, perhaps to mark the first tractor of its kind in the area. (John Topham Picture Library)

page 56 A photograph of modern farm machinery manufactured by Massey-Ferguson who are one of the world's best-known manufacturers of agricultural equipment. (Massey-Ferguson)

Sources of Further Information

PLACES TO VISIT
Many local museums stage exhibits of life on farms in their district, showing past centuries especially in Roman and prehistoric times. There are also quite a number of museums specializing in farming history. One of the biggest is the Museum of Rural Life at Reading. Smaller ones are to be found in many other areas, such as the Abbey Museum at Glastonbury.

Not far from Reading is the Shire Horse Centre at Maidenhead, which specializes in the massive Shire Horses and the work they do, and where you can often see the blacksmiths at work. Some Safari Parks also have sections devoted to farm horses. The Cricket St. Thomas Wildlife Park near Crewkerne, in Somerset, for instance, features the horses themselves, a smithy, waggon-making, and other associated crafts. You will probably be able to find a similar exhibition at a wildlife park in your own district.

Throughout the summer agricultural shows are held in many places, and these are always worth a visit. The biggest is the Royal Show, held at the National Agricultural Centre at Stoneleigh, Warwickshire, in early July. Other big ones are the Royal Highland Show at Edinburgh, the Great Yorkshire Show at Harrogate, the Three Counties Show at Malvern, the East of England Show at Peterborough, and the Royal Bath and West Show at Shepton Mallet. There are many smaller ones as well. Many of these shows stage exhibits of farming in the past as well as today.

In autumn the agricultural shows are followed by Ploughing Matches, which are always interesting for those who like seeing farm horses at work.

During the summer, in almost every county, selected farms hold Open Days, when the public is invited to come along and watch farming operations. You generally ride around the farm on tractor-drawn trailers and are shown the growing crops and the farm animals. Back at the dairy you can watch the milking. Farm Open Days are usually advertised in the local papers and the local libraries. Or you can telephone the local branch of the National Farmers' Union for information about them.

BOOKS
Evans, George Ewart, *Ask The Fellows Who Cut the Hay* (Faber). Information about old-time farming collected by the author in interviews with old countrymen.

Evans, George Ewart, *The Farm and the Village* (Faber).

Seebohm, M. E., *The Evolution of the English Farm* (Allen & Unwin). This book is full of facts.

Trow-Smith, Robert, *English Husbandry* (Faber).

Whitlock, Ralph, *Bulls Through the Ages* (Lutterworth).

Whitlock, Ralph, *Gentle Giants* (Lutterworth). A book about heavy horses on the farm.

Whitlock, Ralph, *The Shaping of the Countryside* (Hale).

Whitlock, Ralph, *A Short History of Farming in Britain* (Ebury Press).

Glossary

Barley: A grain used largely for making into beer.
Corn: Any cereal plant (such as wheat, barley, etc.), or the grain from those plants.
Crossing: Using parents of two different breeds, races, or varieties to produce offspring which inherit the best characteristics of both.
Harvest: The gathering of a ripened crop.
Hay: Grass which has been cut and dried to serve as fodder.
Flail: A tool for threshing grain, consisting of a long handle with a free-swinging bar attached to it.
Fleece: The coat of wool on a sheep, or the coat removed from a sheep by shearing.
Grain: The part of a cereal plant which we eat, usually in the form of flour or breakfast foods.
Industrial Revolution: The period during which Britain (and then other European nations and America) became transformed from mainly agricultural to mainly industrial nations.
Medieval: See *Middle Ages*, below: medieval is the adjective which describes the period of the Middle Ages.
Merchant: A trader; a man who buys and sells goods between one country and another.
Middle Ages: This can mean the period from the fourth to fourteenth centuries but usually, and in this book, it means the period from the eleventh to fifteenth centuries.
Miller: A man who owns a mill, or who works in one, grinding corn into flour.
Peasant: An agricultural labourer or small farmer of humble status.
Reaping: Harvesting a crop of corn.
Rick: A haystack; a stack of hay built in a regular shape, often with a thatched top to keep the rain out.
Scythe: A tool for cutting grass. The handle is held in both hands, and the long curved blade cuts close to the ground in a sweeping movement.
Sickle: A short-handled scythe held in one hand.
Sowing: Planting seed in the ground so that it may grow.
Spinning: Twisting and drawing out fibres of cotton, wool, etc. to make a thread, which is then woven into cloth.
Steer: A castrated bull.
Straw: Stalks of cereal plants after they have been cut. They are used for thatching or plaiting, or as bedding in stables.
Thatch: A roofing material made of reeds or straw.
Threshing: Beating the ripe stalks of corn (with a flail, or in a machine) to separate the grain.
Tractor: A motor vehicle with large rear wheels and deeply treaded tyres, used for pulling heavy loads such as ploughs or harvesters.

Index

agricultural shows 33
Agricultural Workers Union 45
ale 53
America 41, 42–3, 55
apples 19, 21, 23
Arch, Joseph 45
auctions 47
August 9, 11

baling 57
barley 9, 11, 49
barrel-making 23
beans 9
bears 15
Bedford, Duke of 33
beer 49, 53
bees 9, 13, 27, 29
Belgium 17
binders 37
bison 41
blacksmith 15
branding of cattle 41
brewing 49, 53
butter 9, 38–9

cabbages 19
carrots 19
carts 11, 15, 21, 42–3, 51
cats (wild) 15
cheese 9, 39
cherries 19
chestnuts 19
chickens 27
China 17
cider 21, 49
churns 38
Coke, Thomas 33
coopering 23
corn 17, 35
cotton 42–3
cowboys 41
cows 9, 13, 27, 40–41, 46
cream 38–9

crop rotation 33

dairies 27, 38
deer 17
Devon 47
dogs 15, 23, 27
donkeys 23
Dorset 47
drovers 47
ducks 15, 27

eggs 9
emigration 45

fertilizer 11, 33
flails 11
Ford, Henry 55
France 55

gardens 19, 21
geese 9, 15, 27, 47
Germany 15
glass 27
Gloucestershire 47
grain 9, 25
grapes 23
greyhound 23

Hansa Lloyd 55
harrow 13, 15, 31
harvest 11, 21, 23, 37, 42–3
hawks 27
hay 9, 27, 51
haystacks 11, 27, 35, 51
hedging 13
hens 27
herbs 19
Hereford bulls 41
Herefordshire 53
herons 15
Holland 17, 23
honey 9, 13, 29
hops 49, 53
horse-hoe 31

horses 9, 13, 37, 51, 55
hurdle, *see* wicker

June 17, 29, 51
July 29, 51

Kent 53

London 46, 53
lynxes 15

McCormick, Cyrus 37
manors 13, 17, 21, 25
March 9, 11
Massey-Ferguson 57
mattock 11
May 17, 29
Middle Ages 11, 13, 15, 17, 29
milk 39, 51
milking 9, 13, 21, 27
milling 9, 11, 21, 25, 49
monasteries 17, 19
monks 19
mules 43

Netherlands 17, 23
Norfolk 47
Norfolk four-course husbandry 33

oast-houses 53
oats 9
onions 19
oxen 11, 15, 19, 55

parsnips 19
pears 19
peacocks 15
peas 9, 19
pigs 9, 15, 27
plums 19
ploughing 11, 13, 15, 19, 55
poultry 9, 27
prairie 41